Early American Indian Tribes

Marie Patterson, M.S.Ed.

Table of Contents

American Indians

The cultures of the Indian tribes of early America were different from each other. Yet, they all embraced family, food, and shelter as their priorities.

In this book, you will discover the secret chamber of the Southwest Indians. You'll learn about the Feast of the Dead. You may even want to become the "low man on the totem pole"! Try to imagine yourself as a part of each tribe on your journey among the Indians of early America.

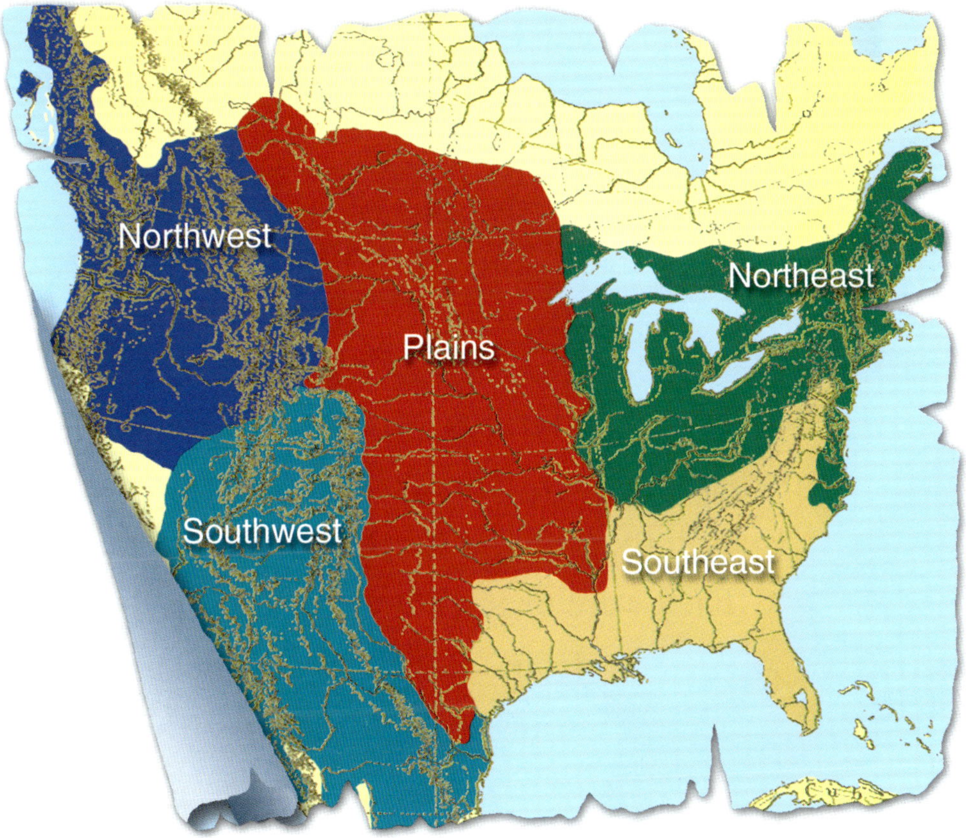

Early American Indian regions ▲

The Woodland People

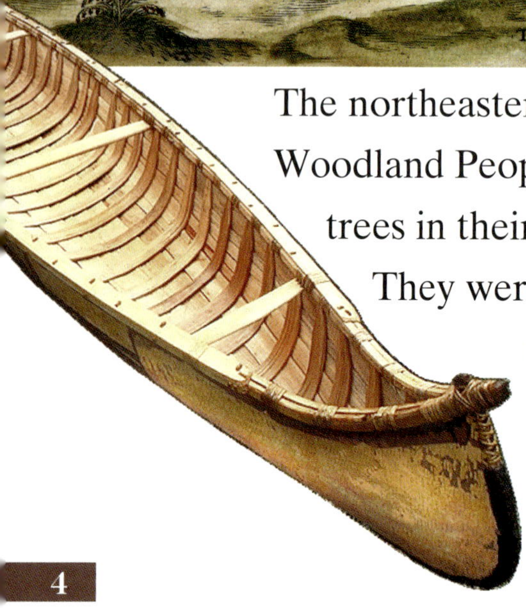

The northeastern tribes were sometimes called the Woodland People. These tribes relied on the many trees in their region for their food and shelter. They were experts at using the wood and bark from trees. They made baskets, canoes, tools, pots, and dishes from wood.

Indians in the Northeast believed it was important to give back to nature. After eating plants or animals, members of these tribes offered a prayer or a **sacrifice** (SAK-ruh-fice) to the land. They might say, "The land gives the people what we need to survive. In return, people should respect nature."

One northeastern tribe, the Huron (HYUR-on), had a special ceremony (SER-uh-mo-nee) to remember those who had died. It was called the Feast of the Dead. Dancing and feasting honored the departed spirits. Sometimes, the ceremony lasted through the night and into the next day.

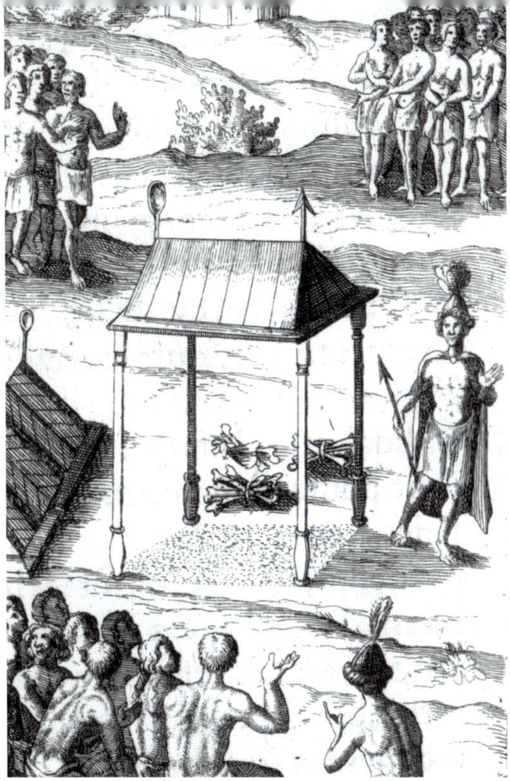

▲ Northeastern burial ceremony

The Wampanoag

The Wampanoag (wom-puh-NO-ahg) tribe helped the Pilgrims survive their first winter by giving them food. These Indians taught the Pilgrims how to grow crops in their new land.

The Art of History

The Indians of the Northeast recorded important events with pictographs (PIK-tuh-grafs). They drew pictures on birch bark scrolls using sharpened bones.

▲ Birch bark pictograph

Life in the Northeast

The Indians in the Northeast lived in villages surrounded by tall **palisades** (pal-uh-SADES), or walls. Most of their homes were **wigwams**, which were only large enough for one family. Wigwams were round-shaped houses that had a smoke hole at the top.

Some tribes lived in **long houses** that were made from bark and poles. Long houses were long buildings with rounded roofs. Several families lived together in each long house.

▼ Algonquin village with palisades and long houses

Many northeastern Indians were farmers who planted crops like tobacco, squash, and yams. Their most important crop was corn.

The tribes used every part of the corn. Women roasted, stewed, boiled, and mashed the kernels.

Sometimes they ground the corn into cornmeal for bread. They even used the husks for crafts, bedding, shoes, and ceremonies.

Mounds of Dead

During the early American period, northeastern Indians began burying their dead in large mounds of dirt. Sometimes the tribe would create many mounds in a row. The picture below shows the Great Serpent Mound in Ohio. The mounds are arranged in the shape of a large snake.

▲ Indian village with birch bark wigwams

Tan That Hide!

Women were in charge of tanning the deer hides to soften the skins. Clothing and shoes were made from the soft skins. Mothers taught the young girls how to tan hides as well as prepare the deer meat for meals.

The Southeast Kinship

Family was very important to the southeastern tribes. Their **kin**, or relatives, were all the people who were related to them on the mother's side of the family. Each family held a set of beliefs that was passed down through the **generations**. They were told who they were going to marry, where they would live, and who their enemies were.

These tribes were **matrilineal** (ma-truh-LIN-ee-uhl). When young couples got married, they lived with the woman's family. Women held places of honor in the tribes. Even though the women were respected, the men still made the most important decisions for the tribes.

The southeastern people believed that all parts of nature had spirits. To show respect for the spirits, they had ceremonies. In each tribe, a **medicine man** or a priest led the ceremonies.

Seminole women making cane syrup

▲ Florida thanksgiving ceremony

Green Corn Ceremony

When the first corn ripened each year, some southeastern tribes held a celebration. They fasted to clean their bodies and spirits. Then, there were feasts and games.

Alligator Wrestling

Alligator wrestling is a Seminole (SEM-uh-nol) tradition. It was a popular sport. They also ate the alligators. This type of wrestling still takes place in Florida today.

Life in a Chickee

Somc of the Indian tribes in the Southeast lived in homes called **chickees**. Chickees were wooden frame homes that were raised off the ground. They were open on all four sides so breezes could blow through the houses. This helped keep the Indians cool during the warm, **humid** summer months.

Other tribes lived in log homes. These buildings helped keep them warm in the winter.

▲ Seminole Indians in front of chickees

When God Roars

Some Indians, like the Cherokee tribe, believed that the sound of thunder was actually a god in the sky.

Members of the tribe were responsible for specific jobs. The women tended the tribe's gardens. Women also made baskets, pottery, and silver jewelry. Men hunted deer, bear, and rabbits. They raised cattle and horses. The men were experts at making weapons, tools, and pipes out of wood. They even built canoes out of tree bark. Young boys learned to catch fish in **weirs**, or underwater traps.

▲ Southeastern Indian village in North Carolina

Early Lacrosse

Among the southeastern tribes, lacrosse was a very popular game. In some ways, it was similar to the sport today. However, each team had 100 players and the game could get very violent. Players often got hurt and some even died during the games.

The Plains People

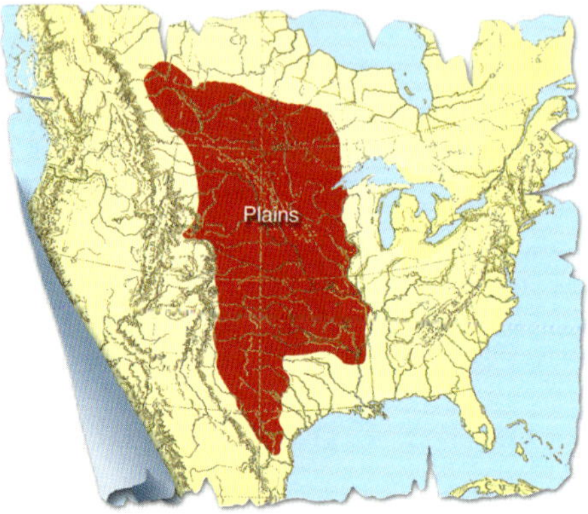

The Plains Indians included about 30 large tribes. They lived in small **bands** so they could move quickly. On the Plains, Indians had to move often to keep safe from their enemies and to find food.

These tribes believed that the whole family should raise the children. This meant parents, grandparents, aunts, and uncles all helped with the children. The families often adopted children who were orphans.

▼ Dog Dance ceremony of a Plains Indian tribe

Music and dancing were an important part of the Plains tribal ceremonies. The Sioux Sun Dance was a way that the Indians gave thanks to the Creator. They believed good things would come to them because of this celebration. They hoped that strength and healing would come to them during the ceremony.

A Robe of Love

It was very common for parents to tell their children whom they had to marry. But, a young man could try to tell his parents whom he wanted to marry. If a man wrapped his robe around a young woman, that meant he loved her.

Dog Lovers

The Plains people used dogs to carry their supplies when moving from one place to another. They strapped frames to the dogs to carry their belongings.

Sioux Sun Dance ▲ ceremony

The Bison Bunch

The Plains people lived in grass houses, **earth lodges**, or **tepees** (TEE-pees). Tepees were very popular because they were easy to pack quickly and move.

Wichita grass house

Dakota tepee

Mandan earth lodge

Indian Sauna

Sweat lodges were built by covering poles with bison hides. Once inside, the men would pour water onto hot stones to make steam. The Indians believed that a sweat lodge purified their bodies and souls.

Frame of a sweat lodge ▶

The men hunted bison and trained the tribe's horses. They protected the tribe, made weapons, and went to war, if necessary. The women on the Plains gathered and cooked the food. They also dried the bison skins. The women watched the children and supervised their daily chores. Women of the tribes enjoyed making crafts like beaded necklaces.

Bison Dung

The Plains Indians used every part of the bison, from its horns to its tail. They even used bison dung. It burned well and made great fuel for their fires.

The thousands of bison on the Plains helped the Indians survive. Everyone helped make different items from the huge animals. Skins were made into blankets and tepee covers. Tools, pots, and shields came from the bison bones. Even the children helped by using bison hair to stuff their toy dolls.

The Desert Dwellers

The Pueblo (PWEB-low) people lived in the Southwest. They believed that people should respect the spiritual world. They also believed that the land was sacred, or holy. They thought there were six cardinal directions—north, south, east, west, above, and below. This included all of nature and the spirit world.

The Squash Blossom Bun

Young women in the Hopi tribe wore their hair in squash blossom buns. They wound their hair around a bent willow stick. It sat in a figure eight over the woman's ears. Today, this hairstyle is only done for ceremonies.

▼ Cliff dwellings built by the ancestors of the Pueblo people

Every Pueblo man belonged to a religious society or group. They held their secret rituals in a **kiva**, or underground room. Women and children could not go into the kivas. Since the Pueblo people were matrilineal, this gave some power to the men. This helped to balance the women's power.

Kachinas

A kachina (kuh-CHEE-nuh) was a messenger between the Zuni people and their gods. During dances and ceremonies, kachina dolls were given to infants, young girls, and women. These gifts were treated with respect and hung in places of honor.

▲ The remains of this kiva no longer include the hard dirt roof and small ladder hole.

The Totem Pole Carvers

The tribes of the Northwest were famous for making totem poles. The poles told family histories and showed social importance in the tribes. Poles had birds, animals, or spirits carved on them. It was actually good to be the "low man on the totem pole." This meant that your job was to carve the lowest part of the pole. Often, the best artist was chosen to carve the bottom of the pole because it was the most visible part.

◀ Different kinds of totem poles in the Northwest

Whale grave totem ▼

Apache woven basket

Basket Case

Women of the Northwest tribes were skilled basket makers. They wove baskets tight enough to hold water. They made coil baskets, purse baskets, and clam baskets. They also made woven mats and wooden boxes.

These tribes believed that nature was a spiritual place. The tribes held ceremonies to show respect for food and weather. The First Foods Ceremony thanked the Creator for their crops. After holding this ceremony in the early spring, the tribes could hunt and gather food.

Party Time!

Northwest Indian families held potlatch parties as a way of showing their importance to the tribe. All the guests received the same gift from the hosts. The gifts could be anything from bracelets to canoes. Sometimes, it took a family many years to plan a potlatch.

A potlatch party in Alaska

▲ Indian women cleaning a beluga whale

Life in the Big House

Northwestern Indians lived in long houses made of red cedar logs. The homes were as large as 60 feet by 150 feet (18 meters by 45 meters). Multiple families lived in each long house. A specially decorated mat told others where each family's assigned living space was located. The outsides of the long houses were painted and decorated. It rains quite a bit in the Northwest, so these buildings were carefully built to keep out the water.

The men rose early to hunt and fish. Boys were taught how to use traps, clubs, and arrows. The women were in charge of cleaning, drying, and cooking the meat and fish.

Hail, Whale!

Northwestern Indians would talk to a whale before harpooning it to show respect to the whale. Then the village honored the whale with singing and dancing. They believed the whale allowed itself to die for the Indians.

▲ This large whale provided many resources to the tribe.

When the Indians **harpooned** a whale, they used every part of it. Everything from the bones to the **blubber** was important to the tribe.

Life has changed over the years within the American Indian communities. But the value of honoring the family remains strong. Many tribes have preserved their ceremonies so that the traditions of their ancestors will be remembered and respected.

Glossary

adobe—river clay found in the Southwest; used to make pueblos

bands—groups of Indians that lived and traveled together

blubber—fatty part of a whale

channeled—made a passageway in dry land to force water to flow in a certain direction

chickees—homes made of palm trees; they were open on all sides to allow breezes to blow through

dung—waste matter from a bison or any animal; manure

earth lodges—large, domed buildings made of poles and packed dirt

fasted—did not eat

generations—members of the same family over time

harpooned—killed with a spear

humid—damp or moist

kin—relatives or family members

kiva—an underground room used by southwestern tribes for secret meetings

long houses—houses with barrel-shaped roofs; many families lived in the same building

maize—corn

matrilineal—tracing a family line on the mother's side

medicine man—important person in a village who studied plants to use for medicine and could lead ceremonies

palisades—tall fences surrounding villages

pictographs—drawings or writings on rocks or bark

potlatch—a party where the hosts give gifts to the guests

pueblos—homes of clay, sandstone, and other natural materials made by tribes of the Southwest

shard—a broken piece of pottery

sacrifice—an offering of something precious to a god

tanning—the process of soaking, drying, and softening an animal skin to make it into leather

tepees—homes made of poles and animal skins

weirs—fences set in streams to trap fish

wigwams—round-shaped homes made with animal skins, bark, and mats made from plants